BACKSEAT TO DRIVER'S SEAT

BECAUSE "WAITING FOR RESCUE" IS NOT A SUSTAINABLE LIFE PLAN

(And No, This Is Not a Book About Cars)

BY
YINKA KUYE-ROMELUS

ISBN **979-8-99485-143-2** (pbk)
ISBN **979-8-99485-141-8** (hcv)
ISBN **979-8-99485-142-5** (ebook)

Library of Congress Control Number: **2026905326**

Dedication

For my daughter, Giselle—my living legacy, my why, and my reason for choosing differently.

And for the little girl in the backseat of a blue Nissan Patrol with white accents, who spent far too long waiting for rescue and finally said, *"Okay, enough waiting,"* took the wheel, and began driving her life with clarity, intention, and **just enough unpredictability** to keep it interesting.

Table of Contents

The Story Begins (With a Little Humor, Because... Life)

I don't remember much about being three years old, but I remember the blue Nissan Patrol with white accents. I remember my mother packing my older brothers and me inside, her face set with determination, and my quiet toddler-level awareness that something dramatic was happening. My memory didn't quite capture whether or not she packed snacks, but the fact that this was a life-changing moment? That was crystal clear.

That moment seared itself into my mind. I often look back on it as a defining pivot in my life's trajectory. I still wonder: what if we had stayed? What would success or failure have looked like for me? Would I have met my incredible husband? Would I have my awe-inspiring daughter? Would my career have unfolded the same way? Would I be happier, or just confused with a different set of problems?

All those questions live in the land of coulda, woulda, shoulda—a place I recommend visiting briefly but not renting an apartment or buying a house in. But the deeper question is this: who would I be if I hadn't been whisked away at such a young age?

Here are the facts: I grew up without a father and, eventually, without a mother. A few years after that dramatic escape, my mother went on a two-week vacation to London and... didn't return for over five years. By the time she reappeared, my brothers and I were in boarding school, fully formed, semi-feral, and figuring out life mostly on our own.

Each passing year came with a ritual of waiting for her to come back. Disappointment gradually hardened into resentment, and resentment eventually numbed into acceptance. Angry at everything and everyone, wishing for something different, I learned very quickly that no one was coming to rescue me. If I wanted a better life, I would have to build it myself, preferably with fewer childhood plot twists.

Looking back now, I see that as the real beginning of my story, the moment that formed my decisions to stop being a passenger and choose to take the wheel instead. The decision to write my own story and live with intention. No more waiting. No more what-ifs. Just a steady focus on *what is.*

I am who I am. I am where I am. And I will always make the best of what is, instead of lingering on what was or spiral over what could have been.

Fast forward forty years, and despite incredibly trying circumstances at multiple life intervals *(the kind that would make great television but terrible actual life)*, I consider myself successful and fully alive.

I'm in a career that I love. I have the most amazing husband, well... most of the time, and a devoted father to our daughter... all of the time. He is, without question, the best life partner I could have ever dreamed up, even on the days when he leaves dishes *"soaking"* in the sink.

The backseat of that Nissan Patrol with white accents, and everything that followed, is simply where my story begins. Because the decision to stop waiting for rescue and choose myself became the quiet thread running through everything that followed: resilience, independence, vision, courage, and faith.

And as you read, I hope you begin to imagine where your own story can go too—ideally with fewer plot twists, but every bit of the courage.

The Choice That Defines Us (Let's Get Into It)

Taking ownership of my direction has been the single most important force in my life. It's the thread running through every decision, every risk, every setback, and every comeback—basically the Wi-Fi signal for my entire personality. It has carried me from living by other people's expectations to building a life that actually reflects who I am... not who everyone thinks I *should* be.

But it didn't start that way.

Like many immigrants, and especially many women, I was taught to value safety above all else. Safety meant gratitude, stability, and silence. *Don't rock the boat. Don't ask too many questions. Be thankful for what you get. Stay in line and you'll be fine.*

Good survival advice? Absolutely.
Good life advice? Questionable at best.

That mindset kept me alive, but it also kept me very, very small. It was the emotionally safe equivalent of sitting in the corner with your hands folded, waiting for permission that never comes.

The turning point came when I realized that survival is not the same as living. That's when I stopped letting fear steer and began paying attention to where I actually wanted to go. And let me be clear: it wasn't one dramatic movie-moment where I stood up and declared, "I choose myself!" No. It was a series of small, stubborn, often uncomfortable choices. Choosing to shed the scarcity mindset, choosing to believe I was meant for more, choosing to take risks even when fear was screaming, *"Girl, sit down!"*

This book chronicles that journey—not just mine, but ours. Because whether you're navigating a career shift, a personal setback, or simply the crushing weight of other people's expectations, you have the same choices I have.

You can let life happen to you, or you can grab the wheel and determine your own path *(ideally with fewer potholes).*

Here's how this book works:

- Each chapter explores a theme of self-determination: resilience, independence, courage, vision, discipline, faith, and legacy.

- I'll share how those themes show up in my life; the good, the hard, the messy, and the *"this should probably be a sitcom"* moments.

- And then, I'll offer **optional** tools, reflections, and prompts you can use to apply those lessons to your own journey...should you choose to—minus the unnecessary detours.

This isn't a book about being perfect. Please. Perfection is exhausting.

This is a book about being persistent.

It's about learning that everything is *figureoutable*—if you're willing to believe it is (and occasionally Google it).

This isn't just a book about where I've been, and it's definitely not here to "inspire" you into buying a vision board or quitting your job and moving to Bali.

It's about making choices with clarity and intentionality— the stuff you actually need to recognize your own power, choose differently, build courage, and move from survival mode to a life that feels fully lived.

My hope is that as you read, you begin to see your own story in these pages. Because taking the wheel and choosing your own direction isn't just my story; it's a universal one.

So let's begin.

And don't worry... no driver's license is required. *(Unless that's already on your to-do list.)*

Chapter 1

Resilience—Standing Tall in Setbacks

Life rarely unfolds in straight lines. It zigzags, spins, doubles back, and occasionally throws you into a ditch for no good reason.

Resilience isn't about pretending the pain doesn't exist; it's about deciding what you're going to do with it. It's choosing: will you let it define you, or refine you? Will you crumble, or will you stand up, dust your shoulders off, and say, *"Okay, well that was rude, but let's keep it moving."*

Funny enough, I didn't learn resilience from books or motivational speeches. I learned it the long, messy, slightly traumatic way—through abandonment, disappointment, and repeated realization that no one was coming to save me.

And while that realization stings, it also hands you something powerful: ownership.

Because when no one is coming, you stop waiting. You stop sitting in the backseat, scanning the road for rescue. You reach forward, grab the wheel, and accept the truth:

if this life is going to move anywhere, it's going to be because *you* decided to drive.

(Fun fact: realizing this early is both devastating and oddly, quite liberating.)

The False Rescue

When I was about twelve or thirteen years old, my mother suddenly returned to Nigeria. And when I say "suddenly," I mean *suddenly*. Like someone opened a door, and boom, there she was, back from her half-a-decade-long "two-week vacation" in London.

By then, my brothers and I had found a steady yet fragile rhythm in her absence. I was in boarding school, fully committed to my accidental orphan storyline: get good grades, get a job, and someday get a life. Nothing fancy. Just survival.

Ambition? Dreams? Luxury items. Definitely not on the roadmap.

Still, I'd managed to carve out a small, functional version of early teenagehood. I'd made two really good friends. I even had a huge crush on a boy. Against all odds, I was starting to get the hang of it.

But when she came back, everything shifted. She was vibrant, dramatic, magnetic, truly the definition of "main character energy" in every room she entered.

And for the first time in years, I felt like I might actually have a mother again. She visited us at school like no time had passed at all, like she had simply stepped away for a long weekend, and somehow... we adjusted. Kids are resilient, or delusional, or maybe both.

Then came the moment: she told us she was taking us with her to London.

We packed our bags like we were auditioning for a commercial: smiling, excited, hopeful.

I remember that day vividly; Mom sweeping into the school like the royalty she was... and still is, announcing the good news.

We piled into the car, drove to the Lagos State airport, and strutted in with our little hearts full of dreams and our bags full of things I'm sure we could have left behind.

And then...disaster.

At the Customs and Immigration desk, something went wrong. Papers shuffled. Voices rose. Confusion thickened. One minute, we were London-bound; the next minute, we were being ushered out of the airport so fast you'd think we were fugitives—not just three kids trying to emigrate with the wrong paperwork.

As we were removed from the airport, I remember thinking how strange it was that no one raised their voice at us directly. There was a lot of tension but no explanation.

No one told us what we'd done wrong. We just followed—because that's what kids do when adults stop explaining things.

I didn't understand it then, and honestly, I still don't fully understand it now. But the dream ended right there. The rescue arc evaporated mid-scene.

A few weeks later, she was gone again. Back to London. And we were left behind. Again.

What followed was a blur: missed schooling for the better part of a year, a return to boarding school after that, and relatives passing us around like a relay baton for the next five years or so. Confusion layered on top of more confusion. Although the details have blurred over time, the ache remained.

That experience forced me to face an uncomfortable truth: my life kept being shaped by other people's decisions. Their choices. Their power. Their whims...hell, their driving skills.Meanwhile, I was just... along for the ride.

And that's when the seed of resilience was planted. I didn't yet have the tools to act on it, but the question began forming quietly:

At what point do I take control of my own life? At what point do I stop waiting for rescue?

I had no answers yet, but I had determination and a growing suspicion that "rescue" might be a myth, like unicorns or reliable Wi-Fi in the middle of nowhere.

Resilience Defined

Resilience isn't about denying pain, it's about refusing to let pain have the last word. It's choosing to stand tall (or at least upright-ish) even when life knocks you down. It's learning to see setbacks not as life sentences but as plot twists, detours, lessons, or even fuel.

Every time I face abandonment, rejection, or disappointment, I have two choices: collapse under the weight of it or rise because of it. And while collapsing is always tempting, rising eventually becomes a habit.

And here's the thing you probably already know:

Resilience is not something you're born with. It's a muscle.

And life, generous as always, will give you plenty of opportunities to work it out.

Reflection Prompts

1. Think of a time when you felt abandoned, disappointed, or let down. How did you respond in that moment?

2. What's one lesson you learned from a setback that still shapes you today?

3. Who are the people in your life who drain your resilience—and who are the ones who help you build and replenish it?

4. Finish this sentence: *"No matter what happens, I will always..."*

Closing Note

That day at the Lagos State airport taught me a painful truth: rescue might not come.

But it also gave me a gift, one wrapped in heartbreak, but a gift, nonetheless.

Because once you learn you can stand back up after disappointment, you stop waiting for someone else to write your story.

You pick up the pen.

You write it yourself.

And honestly? Your plot twists will end up making more sense that way.

Chapter 2

Independence—Owning Your Choices

Independence isn't about doing everything alone. It's about owning your choices, even when they don't make sense to others, or when they disrupt expectations, confuse aunties, or trigger small family conferences.

I've always had an independent streak. Looking back, I actually have to give my mom some credit for this. During the years she *was* around—birth through about seven or eight—she unintentionally trained me to question everything. To push back. To test boundaries. To... inquire. *(Some might call it arguing. I prefer "early leadership development.")*

The Church Incident: My First "Solution"

One of my earliest acts of independence happened at church. I must have been six or seven at the time.

My two older brothers were altar boys, and naturally, I wanted in.

But when I asked, the priests told me I couldn't because I was a girl.

No scripture. No theological explanation. No footnotes. Just simply a hard **"no."**

I wondered why boys could honor and serve God in that way, but girls couldn't? No one could answer that question.

And since no one could make it make sense, I came up with my own solution:

It would simply be easier to be a boy.

So, I acted on it. I threw away all my dresses—literally tossed them over the fence so no one could retrieve them—and I started wearing my brothers' clothes. Then one afternoon, I followed them to the barbershop and had my long hair shaved off. I felt triumphant. I had solved the problem. Access granted. Case closed. My logic was flawless. *(At least to me.)*

My mom was upset, of course. But she didn't shame me. She didn't tell me I was wrong. She didn't crush my spirit in any way.

I remember her just staring at me with the full exhaustion of a woman parenting a child who was clearly **not** following the script. And honestly? She let me explore. That freedom—to question, to act, to make choices—was powerful.

My brothers, on the other hand… got it. They got it *bad.*

She channeled all the frustration she refused to place on me straight into teaching them "responsibility." They should have known better, she said. They should have stopped me from sitting in that barber chair. They should have protected the hair she'd been cultivating for years; the hair she'd prayed for, after raising two boys and finally getting her daughter.

They stood there looking guilty and confused, because truly… what were two preteen boys supposed to do against my level of commitment?

In hindsight, especially in Nigeria in the late '80s and early '90s, there was no language for what I was doing. Gender fluidity wasn't a concept anyone talked about. If modern terminology had existed back then, my family might have assumed I was in a full identity crisis—I'm talking exorcism levels of concern.

But for me, it was never about gender.

It was about **fairness**.

It was about **logic**.

It was about **refusing limitations that made zero sense**.

Throwing my dresses over the fence wasn't rebellion for rebellion's sake. It was my first taste of independence. And it taught me something I've carried into adulthood:

If something doesn't make sense, I don't have to accept it.

Independence, for me, has always meant the courage to question, and the freedom to choose my own response, even if the response is not expected.

The Lesson of Independence

Independence is not about being defiant; it's about being discerning.

It's the ability to think critically, refuse blind obedience, and step outside of "what's expected" so you can live with intention.

Many of us were raised to obey without question. Independence begins the moment you realize that you do have the right to question, and that you have the power to choose differently.

A phrase I use often, personally and professionally, is:

"Make it make sense."

If it doesn't, I will absolutely find another path.

Reflection Prompts

1. Think back to your own childhood: were you encouraged to question rules and expectations,

or taught to simply obey? How has that shaped your sense of independence today?

2. Identify one "rule" you've been following—at work, in relationships, in family life—that doesn't actually make sense to you. Why have you continued to accept it?
   - What would it look like to choose differently in that area? What's one small step you can take to reclaim your independence of thought or action?

3. Who in your life supports your independence, even when your choices confuse them? How can you lean into that support more?

4. Finish this sentence: *"Independence, for me, means..."*

Closing Note

Independence has shaped every choice I've made since those early days. From career decisions to the way I've built my family, I find myself constantly returning to that little girl who threw her dresses over the fence. She reminds me; boldly and with just a touch of defiance, that no one else gets to write my story but me.

Chapter 3

Courage—Fear as a Signal

Fear and I have an understanding. These days, if I don't feel at least a flicker of fear when I'm making an important decision, I double-check my gut. Not because fear should be obeyed, but because it usually means something meaningful is at stake.

Over time, fear stopped feeling like an enemy and started functioning like a signal. At times dramatic, frequently inconvenient, but a useful signal, nonetheless.

Courage, I've learned, isn't the absence of fear. It's the willingness to acknowledge it, name it, and move forward anyway. Some of the biggest breakthroughs in my life didn't happen when I was fearless; they happened when I was terrified and acted anyway.

Fear, when handled correctly, can be a powerful motivator.

One of the hardest decisions I've ever made had nothing to do with money, career trajectory, or immigration paperwork. It was deciding whether to stay or go.

For most of my early adulthood, my plan was straightforward: get an education, work for the United Nations or an international nonprofit, travel constantly, and live out of a suitcase while saving the world with a clipboard and a purpose.

Settling down, getting married, and raising children were not part of that plan. They weren't even adjacent to it. Much less make it onto the vision board.

At the time, I even had a literal "go-bag" in the trunk of my $250 blue Chevy Cavalier. A car so slow and stubborn, I named him Stanley after the character from *The Office*. Stanley wasn't glamorous, but like the sitcom character, he was steady, reliable, and not here for anyone's nonsense.

The go-bag was my constant reminder that the world was waiting, and I was ready to peel out of any situation at twenty-five miles per hour.

But life, as it tends to do, disrupted the plan.

Despite several promising interviews, I kept hitting the same wall: no organization would sponsor my H-1B visa without years of experience. So, I opted for extended graduate school pursuing a master's degree after four years of undergraduate studies and pivoted into temp work just to stay afloat— convinced this was just a temporary detour on the way to something better.

During that time, I was casually dating my now-husband. In my phone, he is saved as "Mandy" short for *Man Candy*. It was fun, light, and deliberately low-stakes. My plan was simple: get the job, grab Stanley and the go-bag, and disappear into a life of global service and airport lounges.

Then came the turning point.

Near the end of my work permit, I came close. Really close. I was deep into the interview process for a position in Liberia, and for the first time in a long while, the future felt tangible.

I remember telling him about the final interview—how confident I felt. How this was the perfect job. How right it all seemed. This was it. This was my launchpad.

He asked a simple question that immediately complicated everything:

"What happens if you get it?"

I answered without hesitation. "Well, I'll be moving to Liberia."

The mood shifted instantly when he asked if I would consider another path—one that involved staying, building something together, and seeing what might be possible.

And just like that, I was paralyzed by fear.

Not because I didn't care—but because I did.

I had built my entire identity around independence and self-sufficiency. Leaving felt familiar. Staying meant vulnerability, compromise, and the uncomfortable reality of choosing connection over escape.

Oddly enough, moving across the world alone felt less risky than staying and letting myself be known. Leaving simply required logistics—visas, flights, paperwork. Staying required vulnerability.

It meant being seen in my uncertainty, my fear, and my unfinished edges—literal and figurative. That kind of exposure felt far more dangerous than any border crossing.

In the end, I stayed. Not because it was romantic or easy—it wasn't—but because it required more courage than leaving would have.

More than a decade later, I can say with clarity: that choice reshaped my life in ways I never could have planned.

Sometimes courage isn't charging toward the life you imagined.

Sometimes it's staying put long enough to build a different one—one that you didn't even know you needed.

Courage at Work

Courage has also shown up in my career. Not through dramatic leaps, but through moments where I had to choose conviction over compliance.

At a prior job, I inherited a senior manager whom leadership had already labeled "overpromoted." Before I had even met her, they wanted me to demote her.

But when I actually worked with her, what I saw wasn't incompetence, it was burnout. A hardworking woman managing an understaffed portfolio under intense scrutiny.

Soon after, I was pulled into an impromptu meeting with the CEO and CFO. You can imagine the intimidation factor of sitting across from those titles when I was merely a director—maybe ninety days into the job. It felt a little like being summoned to the executive equivalent of the principal's office, but with higher salaries and better furniture.

Their message was clear: take action and demote her.

I listened. I breathed. I felt that familiar flicker of fear—the one that signals a crossroads. The kind that tells you a major decision is loading.

Do the easy thing and win favor?

Or do the right thing and risk being unpopular?

When they finished, I calmly said, "I'm still new here, and I can't make that call without more information. I'd like six months to work with her and evaluate the situation myself."

It was **not** the answer they wanted. But courage often looks exactly like that—quiet, steady, and a little uncomfortable.

Six months later, the results spoke for themselves. Together, we stabilized most of her sites and created clear plans for the rest. She has since moved on from that organization—and remains a powerhouse in her own right.

That moment reminded me of something essential: at work, **courage is not defiance, it's integrity**. It's the strength to pause, to question, and to make the decision you'll be proud of later—whether or not it is well-received in the moment.

Reflection Prompts

1. Think about a decision you're avoiding right now because it scares you.

2. What's scarier: making the wrong choice, or staying stuck?

3. Where in your life—personal or professional—are you letting fear drive?

4. What would it look like to treat fear as a compass, not a stop sign?

Closing Note

Fear loves to disguise itself as protection, when more often it's just pointing us toward growth. Courage is the choice to notice that signal, to move forward anyway, and to trust that what's on the other side of fear is freedom.

Chapter 4

Vision—Seeing Beyond What Is

I grew up surrounded by the message that safety was the goal. *Don't rock the boat. Be grateful for what you have. Don't risk what you can't afford to lose.*

Basically: keep your head down, keep your voice low, and keep your dreams...appropriate.

For a long time, I believed that was enough—that surviving was the same as living.

No, it is not.

Vision is what breaks that cycle. Not vision as daydreaming or wishful thinking—but vision as action. Vision is the thing that makes you lift your head from the grind long enough to realize that although you're busy moving, you're not actually *going* anywhere.

Vision refuses to allow *what is* dictate *what will be*. It reminds you that someone else doesn't get to drive forever, unless you keep handing them the keys.

My own turning point came when I was stuck in a mid-level, paper-pushing job that looked impressive on a résumé but felt deeply unsatisfying in real life. I was climbing the corporate ladder, one cautious rung at a time. Following the "safe immigrant playbook": work hard, keep your head down, be grateful for stability, and whatever you do, definitely do not ask too many questions.

And yet, every day, the same thought kept tapping me on the shoulder:

Is this really it? Are we just circling the block now?

That whisper grew louder until I couldn't ignore it. And that's when I created my **Inner Chad**.

Chad, in my mind, represents a very specific man we've all met. The confidently average guy who fails upward, assumes opportunity belongs to him, and never once wonders if he deserves a seat at the table. He just sits down. Sometimes in the wrong chair. Sometimes at the wrong table. But he sits nonetheless, always with confidence.

I have no interest in becoming Chad. But I am fascinated by his certainty.

Chad doesn't wait for directions.

Chad doesn't apologize for taking up space.

Chad assumes that the room—and the road—will simply adjust to him.

So one day, in a meeting where budget and strategy decisions were being made, I asked myself a simple question:

What would Chad do?

Normally, I would have stayed quiet. The safety reflex in me would've said: *don't draw attention. Don't risk sounding wrong. Be grateful just to have a seat at the table—even if the seat is metaphorically a folding lawn chair and completely unstable.*

My voice shook a little, but I spoke. I shared my perspective clearly. And to my surprise, no one rolled their eyes or escorted me out. They actually leaned in. They asked follow-up questions. Some even agreed outright.

That moment wasn't about brilliance. It was about **grabbing the wheel**.

From there, I started bringing "Chad energy" into more spaces—interviews, negotiations, difficult conversations, even family discussions where everyone suddenly remembered I was the youngest and therefore supposed to stay quiet.

And the more I acted from that place of vision, the more doors opened. It wasn't that the world suddenly became more generous; it was that I stopped assuming I needed to shrink to fit inside it.

I began asking different questions:

What if I moved through the world like I was allowed to take up space?

What if opportunity wasn't reserved for "other people," but available to me, too?

That shift was radical. I stopped seeing myself as someone who should be grateful just to be *"in the room where it happens"* and started seeing myself as someone who actually belongs there.

With that came an unexpected relief—the quiet release of pressure I didn't even realize I'd been carrying. The constant self-monitoring. The need to prove I deserved my seat before I could even contribute.

The job didn't change overnight, but *I* did. And that changed everything.

Vision doesn't require a full roadmap. It doesn't need a guaranteed route or perfect timing. It definitely doesn't need a color-coded, cross-referenced five-year plan.

Vision simply asks us to look up and admit that more is possible if we want it.

It asks that we stop staring out the back window long enough to imagine where we actually want to go.

Because the moment you do that, you're no longer just surviving the ride.

You're choosing the direction.

Reflection Prompts

1. Where in your life are you letting "safety" do the driving?

2. If fear wasn't in the passenger seat giving directions, where would you go?

3. Who benefits from you staying in the backseat? Who benefits when you move forward?

4. And if you'd like to, create your own **vision persona**—a version of you who drives with confidence. How do they enter a room? How do they make decisions? Try it on.

Closing Note

The day I stopped silencing that quiet voice and finally listened was the day I moved from the backseat to the Driver's Seat. And once you've driven even a little bit, sitting back and "just surviving the ride" stops being an option.

Survival is sitting still with the engine running.

Vision is putting the car in gear.

And the life you want is up ahead, tapping the dashboard like, *"So…are we going or what?"*

No velvet rope. No VIP list.

Just your hands on the wheel.

Chapter 5

Discipline—Choosing Consistency over Comfort

If resilience is what helps you get back up after life knocks you down, discipline is what keeps you moving forward when nothing exciting is happening. It's the grown-up in the room. The reliable friend. The part of you that whispers, *"Okay, let's try this again,"* even when the rest of you is begging for a nap.

Discipline is *maintenance*. The quiet force behind every transformation. It's not glamorous. It doesn't make a grand entrance like courage or resilience. It shows up in the small, uncelebrated choices: waking up early, showing up when no one is watching, doing the hard thing even when it's wildly inconvenient or unpopular.

For a long time, I thought discipline was punishment. And to be fair, growing up in boarding school did nothing to challenge that belief.

Discipline meant rules, restrictions, consequences, and being told exactly what you *couldn't* do. All girls were required to have no fewer than eight braids in our hair. Lights out was non-negotiable, and holiday "bonus" meant well over a hundred mathematics problems to solve before returning to school.

It definitely was not giving "inspiration"; it was giving "solitary confinement."

But as I got older, I realized true discipline isn't about control, it's actually about **freedom**.

I've come to learn that freedom doesn't come from doing whatever you feel like in the moment. That's not freedom to me, that's chaos. (*Ask anyone who's ever blown a paycheck on trending vibes and then checked their balance the next morning.*)

I believe that freedom comes from structure, from building habits that support your goals, from making a decision and then honoring that decision daily.

My Discipline Practice: Protecting My Energy

One of the most important ways I practice discipline in my professional life is by honoring my need for rest and alignment. That practice didn't come from a wellness podcast or productivity manual – it came from burnout and some hard, honest reflection.

Everyone who's worked with me knows this about me: I build in a mental health break every quarter. Every three months, I pause, recharge, and reset. Not always dramatic, vacation-style trips—sometimes, it's simply a few days of doing nothing, by myself, at home.

It's non-negotiable because I cannot show up as my best if my internal battery is flashing red.

In a prior role, for example, the company couldn't meet my salary requirement. Instead of walking away or settling, I negotiated for something more valuable to me: **four weeks of paid vacation** each year. It wasn't their standard. It wasn't even in their imagination. But because I was clear about boundaries—and consistent in holding them—I got what I asked for.

To me, discipline means knowing your limits and honoring them, even when it feels risky.

My base salary was negotiable.

My need for rest was not.

Discipline also guides how I evaluate my work. Every six months, I pause and ask myself:

Am I still aligned with this company's mission?

Is this role still serving my goals, personally and professionally?

If the answer is yes, I recommit. If not, I initiate a conversation. Sometimes that means recalibrating expectations. Sometimes it means it's time to move on.

That, too, is discipline—choosing alignment over autopilot.

Finally, I establish boundaries early in professional relationships. For example, if I'm contacted after working hours, my first question is always:

"Is this urgent?"

That one question does two things:

It clarifies priorities in the moment, and it trains everyone involved to think through an issue before escalating.

Over time, it becomes a shared time-management tool. Or, as I like to call it, *"a preventive measure against chaos."*

These choices didn't just give me rest; they gave me ownership.

They signaled to everyone around me that sustainability and alignment matter more than blind compliance.

And that, too, is discipline.

Life Time versus Work Time

Discipline doesn't just shape how I work. It also shapes how I show up at home.

When my daughter was around four or five, she started to notice that my life didn't revolve entirely around her. She watched me leave for work each day, and one afternoon she pointed out my two phones and asked what they were for.

I explained that one was for work and the other was for life.

Simple. Clear. Or so I thought.

A few weeks later, while driving her home from school, my work phone rang. I answered it, because of course I did. Mid-call, I glanced at her in the rearview mirror and saw her face cloud over.

After I hung up, she looked right at me and asked:

"Why are you using your work phone during Life Time?"

Listen.

I have received performance feedback from CEOs, boards, and executives.

None of it hit as hard as that one line from a preschooler.

In that moment, she held up a mirror I couldn't ignore. She saw something I couldn't see—that I was allowing work to bleed into the time that should have been ours.

And even at that young age, she understood something I had overlooked: if I could carve out space for work, then surely I could carve out space for life.

From that day forward, I became more disciplined and intentional about protecting our time together. We created "Girls' Night." Every Friday while my husband played tennis, my daughter and I would bake, watch movies, shop, or just chill. No phones, no multitasking, no inbox distractions.

And when plans had to change, I gave her advance notice, and we made a new plan together.

She reminded me that discipline isn't just about work ethic or ambition.

It's about protecting what matters most.

If a four-year-old can understand the difference between "work time" and "life time," then the adults in charge (*me*) can certainly work on honoring it.

Why This Matters

Discipline is not just about working harder.

It is about creating **systems** that keep you aligned with your values, your goals, and your vision.

It's the decision to live intentionally instead of reactively.

Discipline is the bridge between vision and reality.

Vision shows you where you're going.

Resilience helps you get back up when you stumble.

But discipline?

Discipline is what moves your feet, one step at a time, until the vision becomes reality.

Reflection Prompts

1. When you hear the word "discipline," what comes to mind first—punishment, restriction, or freedom? Why do you think that is?

2. Which of your habits move you closer to your goals, and which ones quietly pull you away?

3. How often do you pause to reassess whether your current work, relationships, or other commitments still serve your long-term goals?
   - What might change if you made this a regular practice?

4. How do you show the people who matter most that their time with you is sacred? Where might you need stronger boundaries?

Closing Note

Discipline hasn't just shaped my career; it has reshaped my home. It's not just about carving out breaks from work or building systems to stay aligned. It's about choosing presence when it matters most.

That day in the car, when my daughter asked, *"Why are you using your work phone during Life Time?"* I must admit, I was a little salty.

Children have a talent for delivering performance reviews with zero filter and one hundred percent accuracy. She wasn't just calling me out; she held up a mirror I didn't exactly ask for, but absolutely needed, and it became an unexpected moment of clarity and recalibration.

Her question reminded me that discipline isn't only about what you achieve, but also about how you honor what you love. It's consistency in the values you claim, not just the tasks you complete.

Because at the end of the day, success without presence is just burnout driving a nicer car and wearing more expensive clothes.

Discipline, however, when practiced with intention, is what ensures you don't miss the moments that make all the hard work worth it.

Chapter 6

Faith—The Anchor Within

Faith isn't blind optimism, it is steadiness. It's not "good vibes only" or pretending everything is fine when it clearly is **not**. Faith is the quiet conviction that no matter how uncertain the road ahead looks, something steady is carrying you forward—even if the GPS is glitching.

I haven't always had faith in people. In fact, I used to confidently state, *"I don't like people."*

For me, trust has always been something that must be earned. Given my childhood and the disappointments that came early and often, most people started at a disadvantage—met with quiet skepticism and the lingering sense that it was only a matter of time before they revealed themselves.

However, as I've grown into what I like to call my *"big age"* (anything over forty) I've refined that position.

Now I say, boldly and with my whole chest:

"I only like the people I like."

That shift happened because I realized something surprising: I actually *do* have faith in people—not in all of humanity *of course*, but in the select few I've chosen to allow into my circle. The people I've grown to like... and love. The ones who have earned my trust instead of demanding it.

But beyond people, I also have faith in the divine. I firmly believe we all each carry divine favor, that each one of us is here for a reason, and that something bigger than us is giving us a gentle (and sometimes not-so-gentle) push in the right direction. We may not always understand it in the moment, but faith means trusting the nudge.

My faith has been tested often. As a Black woman in professional spaces, I've had to live with the reality that many people don't believe I should have the success I've achieved. And even when they accept it, I'm often labeled the "exception," as if being excellent was some kind of cosmic accident.

That's why I've had to cultivate faith in **myself**. Faith that by telling my story and showing up fully, I can help shift that narrative. My prayer now is that what they call an *"exception"* today will one day become the rule. Not just for me, but for my daughter and for generations of brilliant Black women who are tired of being the outliers in rooms they belong in.

Faith has carried me through every abandonment, every disappointment, every moment when I thought the ground had disappeared under my feet. When my parents weren't there, faith whispered, *"You'll survive this."* When doors closed, faith rolled her eyes and said, *"Get up. There's a window over there."*

And through it all, I have never seen failure as the end. Every unsuccessful thing has always sparked the next adventure. That, to me, is the essence of faith: knowing your possibilities are endless—even when your present circumstances are giving *"Nope! Not today."*

A Leap of Faith at Work

Faith has also shaped my career in ways I never expected. I remember leaving a "safe" role where the salary was steady, the benefits were solid, yet the work was…quietly, relentlessly soul-snatching.

If I had to send one more proposal about adopting new technology in leasing—only to watch it crawl through layers of bureaucratic red tape inside a mammoth organization, ultimately going nowhere in favor of "policy" and paper-shuffling—I would have lost my mind.

Deep in my spirit, I knew staying would suffocate me.

So, I did something that made no sense on paper: I moved into an untested role at a start-up tech company with five employees and a dream.

I felt wildly unqualified. What did I really know about technology or building a company from scratch? The imposter syndrome was loud. It had a microphone. It had slides. It had receipts.

As an immigrant woman of color, people expected me to cling to stability—to hold on to a paycheck like it was oxygen, even if the job itself drained the life out of me. But I chose differently.

I chose faith.

Faith in myself.

Faith in whatever possibilities were waiting around the corner.

And that choice paid off. Within weeks, I proved my value to the team and to myself. The "safe" path had promised me stability, but faith gave me freedom.

Faith doesn't always mean praying for something to fall into your lap. Sometimes it means stepping away from something that's killing your spirit, even if you can't yet see what's waiting on the other side.

The Lesson of Faith

Faith doesn't guarantee a perfect outcome. Let's be clear.

What it *does* guarantee is momentum. It keeps you moving, believing, and discovering what's possible even when your present reality is trying to tell you otherwise.

Faith is the agreement you make with yourself, and with the divine, that your story isn't finished even when things fall apart.

Reflection Prompts

1. Do you see faith as rooted in God, the universe, people, or yourself? Where does your anchor sit?

2. Think of a time when your faith was tested. What did you learn from how you responded?

3. What story are you telling yourself about your future right now? How would faith rewrite that story?

4. Finish this sentence: *"Even when I can't see the next step, I trust that..."*

Closing Note

I've had faith in myself and in the divine even when others were still squinting to see it.

I've had faith in my survival, even in the quietest moments of abandonment.

And after every disappointment, I've believed that there was something ahead worth moving toward.

Faith has proven me right. Sometimes loudly, sometimes with a side-eye, but always in alignment with where I was meant to go.

Chapter 7

Legacy—Leaving More than You Take

Legacy isn't about statues, wealth, or fame.

And let's be honest: most of us aren't getting a statue anyway (and even if we did, someone would eventually graffiti it, climb it for Instagram, or pee on it after a night out...and that's before we even get into the maintenance fees; *but I digress*).

Legacy is about impact.

It's the fingerprints you leave on people's lives, the ideas that outlive you, and the doors you hold open so the folks behind you don't have to kick them down.

For much of my life, legacy felt like a luxury. I wasn't thinking about what I'd leave behind; I was thinking about how to make it to next week, next month, next year.

After undergrad, I worked as a seasonal cashier at a casino because no company in my field would sponsor an H1-B without prior work experience. During graduate school, I survived on temp jobs—not because they were aspirational, but because they were flexible and kept me afloat.

For a long time, survival *was* the legacy. I was always preparing an exit strategy, ready to hit the road and leave everything behind if I had to.

Until I faced a different fear: staying.

Staying and figuring it out without a guaranteed rescue plan.

For a long time, I thought survival was enough.

It isn't.

Survival is the prologue.

Legacy is the story.

Legacy at Home

When I think of legacy now, I think first of my daughter. I think about the world she will inherit, and the example I'm setting for her every single day.

I don't want her to grow up in a world where she is treated as an "exception." I want her to grow up in a world where her brilliance is assumed. Where her independence isn't questioned. Where her courage isn't rare—but expected.

Legacy doesn't just move forward; it also flows backward. It connects us to the generations that shaped us—even in complicated ways.

I think about my mother. On some subconscious level, I am her legacy, just as I hope to be my daughter's. And through years of therapy and soul-searching, I began to understand the throughline between how deeply I love my mother, how fiercely I resented her, and how determined I am not to become her.

Yet, as an adult and a mother myself, I see her differently now. I can understand and accept the decisions she made that shaped me. The abandonment I felt as a child, I now see as her own survival mode. Perhaps, she was not in control of her choices, and survival required sacrifice. Today, I can ask myself honestly: *if I were in her shoes, what choices would I have made?*

I am both shaped by her absence and inspired by her resilience. In many ways, I am her legacy, and in just as many, I've worked hard to rewrite it.

Legacy at Work

Legacy has also shown up in my work. Not in what I've achieved for myself, but in what others have seen reflected in me.

For years, I walked into rooms where I was the only one who looked like me. I've been dismissed, underestimated, and treated as though my presence needed a slide deck and footnotes explaining why I belonged there.

The awkward introductions. The looks. The questions. All of it was telling.

I remember sitting in a meeting when another leader casually shared that she'd been approached to invest in a startup—and had passed on the opportunity. When I mentioned that I was actually an investor myself, her reaction said everything.

She looked genuinely surprised. Not curious. Not impressed. Just surprised—as if the idea that *I* could be an investor hadn't even registered as a possibility. Her face betrayed a quiet disbelief that lingered a moment too long.

Instead of shrinking, I did the opposite. I leaned in, showed up clearer, and more fully myself. I shared my story. I advocated for myself, and just as intentionally now make it a point to pull other women up, because no one thrives alone.

I champion other people's ideas in rooms where they aren't present, proving through action that leadership doesn't have one face or one voice.

I didn't always recognize the impact in real time. I remember presenting with the executive team at my prior company's annual meeting. Later that night, while waiting at the bar, a Black woman approached me and shared how proud she felt seeing me up there with the rest of the leadership team.

For her, it wasn't just another presentation; it was evidence. Evidence that someone who looked like her could take up space at the top in an industry where Black women are usually confined to the bottom of the totem pole.

At the time, I didn't think of myself as a role model. I thought I was just doing my job. But in retrospect, that moment shifted something in me. What felt ordinary to me was revolutionary to her.

That's legacy, too. The kind that sneaks up on you simply because you decided to exist boldly and show up as yourself.

Now I know that whenever another woman of color sees me in a leadership role, something clicks for her:

She doesn't have to twist herself into someone else's mold to lead.

She can lead as herself.

That is legacy. Rewriting the narrative so the next person doesn't have to fight the same battles. Until one day, the "exception" becomes the rule.

Legacy Expanded

Legacy starts at home, but it doesn't stop there. It spills into our communities, our cultures, and the generations we may never meet.

My legacy isn't just about me, my daughter, or my mother. It's about every person, every woman, and anyone who sees a piece of themselves in my story and dares to believe they can write their own.

Legacy is shifting the narrative from scarcity to abundance, from invisibility to presence, from surviving to being so fully alive that others feel permission to do the same.

Legacy is the wild realization that your life is bigger than your goals and your to-do lists.
It's planting seeds you may never see grow, and doing it anyway, because the future deserves it.

The Lesson of Legacy

Legacy isn't a single moment, it's mileage. It's the accumulation of resilience, independence, courage, vision, discipline, and faith; lived consistently over time.

It's not about perfection, it's about persistence.

Legacy is the story people will tell because of the way you lived, not because you planned a dramatic exit.

Reflection Prompts

1. What do you want people to say about you when you're not in the room?

2. If you could pass down one lesson to the next generation, what would it be?

3. Think about your daily choices: are they building the legacy you want to leave?

4. Finish this sentence: *"My legacy will be..."*

Closing Note

Legacy isn't a future project. It's happening right now, whether you're paying attention or not.

Every time you choose courage over comfort, presence over autopilot, intention over obligation—it counts.

Your legacy is being shaped in real time by how you show up.

So the only question left is: *are you steering it, or just along for the ride?*

From Backseat to Driver's Seat—Keys in Hand. Engine On. Your Move.

When I look back on my journey—from that little girl staring out the back window of a blue Nissan Patrol with white accents to the woman writing this book—one truth rises above everything else:

We always have a choice.

We may not control the circumstances we're born into. We may not control the losses, the disappointments, or the wildly unqualified opinions people try to project onto our lives.

But we *do* control how we respond.

We control the vision we hold for ourselves. The resilience we summon when life decides to get creative. The discipline we bring to our habits. The independence we claim in our decisions. The courage we lean into when fear whispers, *"No ma'am, not you, not today. Sit down."* The faith that carries us when we can't see the next step. And the legacy we choose to leave behind instead of one that was slapped on us by default.

That is what it means to move into the Driver's Seat.

It's not about perfection. Perfection is a scam and a headache. It's about persistence, the quiet kind that doesn't need applause.

It's not about having it all figured out. *Who does? Show me one person.*

It's about taking one step at a time, guided by the belief that your story is worth writing—on your terms, in your voice, with whatever pen (or car) you can currently afford.

The Driver's Seat isn't reserved for the boldest, the loudest, or the luckiest. It's available to all of us, at any moment, through the choices we make.

You don't have to wait until you feel ready.

You don't need all the answers.

You don't even need confidence or a driver's license. The car starts without it.

You just need to decide to stop sitting in the backseat of your own life.

And yes, you'll have to decide again tomorrow. And the day after. That's the whole point.

Because moving into the Driver's Seat isn't a destination, it's a decision. A daily commitment to drive your story instead of being chauffeured around by fear, expectations, or history.

And sometimes, the reminder comes from unexpected places. Like the day my daughter looked at me from the backseat, her eyes full of confusion and innocence, asking why I was using my work phone during "Life Time."

In that moment, she didn't just call me out, she called me *forward*—back into the Driver's Seat.

So as you close this book, I invite you to ask yourself:

What time is it? Is it Work Time, Fear Time, Survival Time, or Life Time?

And are you in the backseat—or the Driver's Seat?

Because what began for me in the backseat continues here—with the keys in hand and the wheel firmly held.

Direction chosen.

Legacy claimed.

And a story no longer waiting for permission—fully, un-apologetically written, owned, copyrighted, and trade-marked by me.

And yes.

I'm driving.

Your Invitation (Should You So Choose)

I invite you to pause and ask yourself:

- What vision do I dare to claim?

- Where can I practice resilience instead of giving up?

- What habits of discipline will actually sustain me?

- How will I own my independence today, even in the small things?

- What courageous step am I avoiding, and what happens if I just...take it?

- Where will I choose faith instead of fear?

- And what legacy am I building right now, through the tiny choices of this day?

Don't just skim those questions.

Answer them.

Write them down.

Let them shape your next step.

Because moving into the Driver's Seat doesn't begin "someday."

It begins **now**.

Acknowledgments

No story is written alone, and this book is no exception.

First, to my husband—my partner in every sense of the word. Thank you for loving me, challenging me, grounding me and holding me steady when my courage wavered and my ideas ran a little too fast. You have been my sounding board, my balance, and my reminder that love itself can be an act of choosing—daily, intentionally, and with humor.

To my daughter—my living legacy. Every word I've written here is, in some way, a love letter to you. Thank you for showing me daily what it means to see the world with curiosity, honesty, and zero tolerance for nonsense. You are the reason I insist on leaving the world better than I found it. And also the reason I now understand the phrase *"Life Time"* with great seriousness.

To my mother—for shaping me, even in ways I only came to understand later. Our complicated journey has been one of my greatest teachers. Thank you for passing on your fire, your independence, and your survival instinct. I am my mother's daughter. And I carry both what you gave me and what I chose to transform.

To my brothers—my first companions in both mischief and resilience. Thank you for showing me that I could be a girl and still be "one of the boys." Thank you for being the constants in a life that changed often. You taught me early how to stand my ground, and occasionally how to dodge consequences.

To my uncle and surrogate dad—thank you for locating us in Nigeria through what can only be described as divine intervention mixed with detective work. Thank you for rescuing us from a multiverse clearly scripted by Chaos itself, and for deciding correctly that therapy was **not optional**, even when I had no idea why. Without you, the emotional damage would have been... let's just say well above recommended levels.

To my in-laws—thank you for accepting me into the clan and providing the stability, unconditional love, and unwavering support I was too afraid to even know I needed. In you, I learned that family can also be chosen and expanded.

To the mentors, friends, and colleagues who believed in me even when I didn't fully believe in myself—your encouragement helped me see what was possible. Thank you for opening doors, for sitting with me in my doubts, challenging me when necessary, and for reminding me that no step forward is ever too small.

To every person, woman, and woman of color who has ever felt unseen, underestimated, or told that her place was at the margins: this book is for you. May my story remind you that your voice matters, your choices matter, and your life is yours to drive.

Appreciation to ChatGPT (OpenAI, 2025) for its co-pilot support on clarity, flow, and light copy edits. But let's keep it real: I'm still steering and driving. ChatGPT just stopped my punctuation, especially the commas and apostrophes that were out here freelancing, from committing grammatical crimes.

And finally, to you, the reader—thank you for opening these pages and riding along with me. My hope isn't just that you see *me* in these words, but that you see yourself. Capable. Clear. And fully qualified to write a story that is unapologetically yours.

If you'd like to stay connected or see what I'm working on next, you can find me here:

Website: www.yinkakuyeromelus.com
Instagram / LinkedIn: @yinkakuye

No pressure. No performance.
Just a place to connect—if it feels right.

Appendix

My Answers

Notes from the Driver's Seat

These are my answers to the reflection prompts throughout this book.

Not because they're the right answers.
Not because they're complete.
And not because they're meant to replace your own.

They're simply how I answered these questions at this point in my life, with the perspective I have now.

Some answers feel settled. Others are still evolving. And a few surprised me as I wrote them.

You don't need to read this section in order.
You don't need to read it at all.

But if you're curious how these questions landed for me, this is where I parked my thoughts.

On Resilience

Prompt: *Think of a time when you felt abandoned, disappointed, or let down. How did you respond in that moment?*

I handled it on my own.
I didn't wait.
I didn't ask for help.
I moved forward assuming I was on my own.

Self-reliance always protected me, until it didn't.

What I've had to learn much later is that resilience isn't just about standing up alone. It's also about knowing when to lean in and lean on a trusted circle without feeling weak.

I'm still practicing that part.

Prompt: *What's one lesson you learned from a setback that still shapes you today?*

That disappointment doesn't require closure to move on.

Some things never get explained. Some people never circle back. Some endings don't arrive neatly wrapped. Waiting for resolution can quietly keep me stuck.

For me, moving forward doesn't always require complete understanding. Sometimes it just means deciding to move.

Prompt: *Who are the people in your life who drain your resilience, and who are the ones who help you build and replenish it?*

People who require me to perform, shrink, or over-explain drain me.
People who confuse access with entitlement drain me.

The people who replenish me are steady. They don't rush my process or demand versions of me I've already outgrown. They let me be quiet when I need to be quiet, and honest, even when honesty is inconvenient.

Prompt: *Finish this sentence: "No matter what happens, I will always..."*

No matter what happens, I will always choose clarity over chaos.

I may not always choose comfort. I may not always choose the easiest path. But I will always choose to be honest with myself about where I am, what I need, and what I'm no longer willing to tolerate.

That choice has served me well thus far.

On Independence

Prompt: *Think back to your childhood: were you encouraged to question rules and expectations, or taught to simply obey? How has that shaped you?*

I was encouraged, sometimes accidentally, to question. Not always safely. Not always with permission. But questioning was never discouraged enough to stop me.

That shaped me into someone who notices inconsistencies quickly. I don't accept rules just because they exist. I want them to make sense.

That instinct followed me into adulthood and has made me very *"fun"* at meetings.

Prompt: *Identify one "rule" you've been following that doesn't actually make sense to you.*

For a long time, I followed an unspoken rule that gratitude required silence.

That if I was fortunate enough to be included, I should stay agreeable, speak carefully, take up less space, and avoid rocking the boat—even when the boat was already taking on water.

I followed that rule longer than I should have.

Prompt: *What does it look like to choose differently in that area?*

It looks like speaking even when my voice shakes.
Asking the question without always softening it first.
Allowing myself to be seen as direct instead of palatable.

This has occasionally made people uncomfortable.
But for me, it's been freeing.

Prompt: *Who in your life supports your independence, even when your choices confuse them?*

The people who don't need to fully understand my decisions to respect them.

They ask questions without issuing warnings. They trust my judgment even when they wouldn't make the same choice themselves.

And they don't start sentences with, "Are you sure you want to do that?"

Prompt: *Independence, for me, means...*

Owning my decisions without outsourcing responsibility for the outcome.

It doesn't mean I don't ask for advice.
It means I don't pretend someone else is driving when I'm the one holding the wheel, especially when I already know where I'm going.

On Courage

Prompt: *Think about a decision you avoided because it scared you.*

Staying.

Leaving has always been easier for me. I know how to pack, pivot, and start over. Staying, especially in situations that require vulnerability, always feels risky.

Apparently, commitment is a scarier adventure.

Prompt: *What's scarier: making the wrong choice, or staying stuck?*

Staying stuck.

Wrong choices always teach me something. Staying stuck quietly teaches me to doubt myself.

And doubt has been much harder to unlearn.

Prompt: *Where in your life are you letting fear drive?*

Whenever I delay a hard conversation, I already know I need to have.

Fear doesn't usually stop me from acting, it slows me down just enough to make inaction feel reasonable.

Prompt: *What would it look like to treat fear as a compass, not a stop sign?*

It looks like paying attention instead of constantly pulling over.

Usually, it starts with one uncomfortable, double-sided question: *what's the worst that could happen, and what am I afraid will be revealed if I do this?*

The answer tends to be annoyingly informative and almost always points me toward forward motion.

On Vision

Prompt: *Where in your life are you letting "safety" do the driving?*

Every time I stay somewhere out of habit instead of alignment.

For me, safety is subtle. It disguises itself as logic, timing, patience, *"let's just wait and see."*

Very convincing.

Prompt: *If fear wasn't in the passenger seat, where would you go?*

Toward work that feels expansive instead of merely impressive.
Toward conversations I've postponed.
Toward choices that feel honest, even when they're inconvenient.

I also would have produced my podcast and published this book a lot sooner.

Prompt: *Who benefits from you staying in the backseat? Who benefits when you move forward?*

Other people's comfort benefits when I stay still.
Other people's expectations benefit.
Old narratives benefit.

When I move forward, I benefit. My family benefits.

On Discipline

Prompt: *When you hear the word "discipline," what comes to mind, and why?*

Structure.

For a long time, discipline felt like restriction. Now it feels like protection, the kind that keeps me aligned instead of reactive.

It's less about willpower and more about boundaries.

Which I learned the hard way.

Prompt: *Which habits move you closer to your goals, and which quietly pull you away?*

Protecting my energy moves me closer.
Overcommitting pulls me away.

Burnout doesn't announce itself loudly. It shows up disguised as productivity and usefulness. I've learned to be suspicious of both.

Prompt: *How often do you pause to reassess whether your current work, relationships, or commitments still serve your long-term goals?*

Regularly.

Not on a spreadsheet. Not with a ceremony.
Just honest check-ins that usually start with: *is this still making sense?*

Sometimes the answer surprises me.

Prompt: *What might change if you made this a regular practice?*

I waste less time trying to justify things that no longer fit.
I stop confusing momentum with alignment.

Prompt: *How do you show the people who matter most that their time with you is sacred?*

By being present.
By not multitasking them.
By honoring "Life Time" the same way I honor work commitments, without apology.

It turns out attention is a discipline too.

On Faith

Prompt: *Do you see faith as rooted in God, the universe, people, or yourself?*

All of the above, in different measures, at different times.

For me, faith is less about certainty and more about steadiness, about continuing forward even when clarity is incomplete.

Prompt: *Think of a time when your faith was tested. What did you learn?*

That faith doesn't eliminate fear; it coexists with it.

Faith gives me a reason to keep moving when fear shows up.
I learned that waiting for certainty is optional.

Prompt: *What story are you telling yourself about your future right now? How would faith rewrite that story?*

I don't need all the answers before I move.

Faith rewrites the story by reminding me that progress still counts, even when clarity is incomplete.

Prompt: *Finish this sentence: "Even when I can't see the next step, I trust that..."*

I'll recognize it when it appears.

On Legacy

Prompt: *What do you want people to say about you when you're not in the room?*

That I was clear.
That I was kind.
That I didn't shrink myself just to make things easier for others.

That I left things better than I found them.
And that I made space for someone else to do the same.

Prompt: *If you could pass down one lesson to the next generation, what would it be?*

You don't need permission to choose yourself.

Prompt: *Think about your daily choices: are they building the legacy you want to leave?*

Some days, yes. Some days, not yet.

Legacy isn't built in grand gestures. It's built in the quiet decisions I make when no one is watching and when no one is applauding.

Prompt: *Finish this sentence: "My legacy will be..."*

It's too soon to tell.

But my hope is that I stay consistently in the Driver's Seat and make it easier for others to do the same.

Closing Note

This appendix isn't a conclusion. It's a snapshot.

These answers will change. I hope they do.

And when I read this section at a different stage of life and feel differently, I'll take that as proof that I'm still driving, still choosing, still paying attention.

I'm allowing myself some grace.

And that is a legacy I can live with.

About the Author

Yinka Kuye-Romelus is an author, storyteller, and operations executive known for transforming complexity into clarity—both on the page and in practice. Born in Nigeria and raised across continents, her life has been shaped by resilience, reinvention, and an early understanding that waiting for rescue is rarely a viable strategy—unless you're a princess in an earlier generation of Disney movies.

She holds a **master's degree in Political Science from Northeastern University** and a **bachelor's degree in Communications and Business Administration from Eastern Connecticut State University**. With more than a decade of leadership experience in the multifamily and prop-tech industries, Yinka has built and scaled teams, challenged systems that no longer serve, and led with a steady blend of strategic rigor and emotional intelligence.

She is also the creator, writer, and producer of ***Filed & Deranged: Property Management's Classified Circus***, a mock–true-crime comedy podcast inspired by real industry incidents and human unpredictability. Her storytelling is marked by sharp observation, dry humor, and a refusal to romanticize survival.

Backseat to Driver's Seat is her debut book—a concise, reflective guide to choosing direction, reclaiming agency, and building a life that feels fully lived.

Yinka lives in Massachusetts with her husband, daughter, and dog. Where "Life Time" is treated as seriously as any meeting on the calendar.